BAVARIAN MOTOR WORKS (BMW) - A PRODUCTION SURVEY

Reported by

Cmdr. H.C. HASKELL, USNR
NavTecMisEu

CIOS Target Nos. 5/2, 5/64, 5/168, 26/1, 26/72, 26/79 & 26/156
Jet Propulsion
Aircraft Engines

COMBINED INTELLIGENCE OBJECTIVES SUB-COMMITTEE
G-2 Division, SHAEF (Rear) APO 413

RESTRICTED.

The Naval & Military Press Ltd

Published by

The Naval & Military Press Ltd
Unit 5 Riverside, Brambleside
Bellbrook Industrial Estate
Uckfield, East Sussex
TN22 1QQ England

Tel: +44 (0)1825 749494

www.naval-military-press.com
www.nmarchive.com

In reprinting in facsimile from the original, any imperfections are inevitably reproduced and the quality may fall short of modern type and cartographic standards.

BAVARIAN MOTOR WORKS (BMW) - A PRODUCTION SURVEY

SUMMARY

With especial consideration to the problems encountered in tooling for mass output, model changes including the turbo-jet conversion program, and how the company attempted to meet the problem of Strategic Bombing.

June 1945

TABLE OF CONTENTS

		Page
1.	Introduction	6
2.	Executive Personnel	6
3.	History 　　BMW 132 　　BMW 801 　　PLW 003 　　Intake Ducts	9
4.	Future Plans	18
5.	003 Production Engineering and Design Limitations 　(a) Design Limitations 　(b) Production Engineers in Design Liaison 　(c) Turbine Bucket 　(d) Nozzles 　(e) Turbine Wheel Changes in Field 　(f) Spare Parts and Spare Units 　(g) Volksjaeger (He-162)	19 19 19 21 21 21 21 21
6.	Design Highlights 　(a) 003 A-2 Turbojet 　(b) 018 Turbojet 　(c) 028 PTL Gas Turbine	22 22 32 44
7.	Production Trends 　(a) Program Changes 　(b) "Going Underground" 　(c) Parabolic Sawtooth Buildings 　(d) Decision to Move 003 Production Underground 　(e) Decision to convert all fighters to jets 　(f) Salt Mine Problems	44 44 44 45 45 45 45

TABLE OF CONTENTS (cont'd)

		Page
8.	Salt Mines as Factories	50
	(a) Access, Corrosion	50
	(1) Eisenach Area Mines	50
	(2) Nordhausen Mines	50
	(3) Stassfurt Mines	50
	(4) Value of Underground Dispersals	50
9.	Test Stands	51
10.	Employment Policy	51
11.	Production Schedules	51
	(a) "K" Programs – Production Schedules	51
	(1) Trend	60
	(2) 003 Turbojet Program 9-11-44	61
	(3) 003 Turbojet Program 3-8-45	62
12.	Junker 004 vs. BMW 003	62
13.	Government Supervision	63
	(a) Accounting and Records	63
	(b) Machine Tool Allocations	63
14.	Items of Varied Interest	63
	(a) Forged Cylinder Heads	63
	(b) Impellers	63
	(c) Cylinder Finning	65
	(d) Altitude Chamber	65
	(e) "Solid" Cement Factories	65
	(f) Crankshaft, Rods; Vibration Dampner	65
	(g) "Idiots Control"	65
15.	Conclusions	65

Figure 1. Director in Chief, Wilhelm Schaaf.

Figure 2. Director of Production Fattler.

BAVARIAN MOTOR WORKS (BMW) - A PRODUCTION SURVEY

1. **Introduction.**

(a) The BMW plants other than the destroyed and unavailable factories in the Berlin area were visited during the first three weeks of May 1945. Top personnel in close touch with the Air Ministry were interrogated and documents studied.

(b) Special notice has been given to the production and plans for both production and development of turbojets, and how these plans were linked to aircraft production and design.

2. **Executive Personnel.**

(a) Executive personnel consisted of those that were located and interrogated, and those that were not available but were important cogs in the organization. With one exception it is believed that every key executive was contacted.

(b) Director in Chief, Wilhelm Schaaf.

In charge of top policy. Claimed not to have been a member of Nazi Party, but served under Minister of Production, Albert Speer, from 1942 to 1944 as Industrialist in Charge of Automotive Equipment. (Figure 1)

(c) Eisenach Area Director of Production Fattler. (Figure 2)

This executive is a brilliant production engineer and organizer. He worked in the United States for three (3) different intervals, aggregating some fifteen (15) years, and as an engineer for Ford, Chevrolet and Taft Pierce. He was thoroughly versed in volume production technique and was largely responsible for the refinement of turbojet design into an extremely practical production proposition. He claimed to have made about five (5) trips to the Mittelwerke in Nordhausen. Evidence indicates that he was probably an unofficial production advisor to the Mittelwerke, as well as a member of the Nazi party.

2. Executive Personnel (cont'd)

(d) Director Max Fritz, Eisenach.

In charge of reciprocating engine design. Conducted negotiations with Mr. Mead of Pratt and Whitney concerning license to produce early the "Hornet" and "Wasp" engines.

(e) Director (of **all** production) Stoffregel.

Formerly of Berlin and temporarily living in Stassfurt. Claimed not to have been a member of the Nazi party. (He appears in the left background of Figure 3 taken at the elevator pit entrance of the New Stassfurt Salt Mine Plant.)

(f) Doctor Oestrich (foreground of Figure 3).

In charge of all turbojet (TL) and gas turbine (PTL) design and development. He was formerly from Berlin and temporarily located at Stassfurt. An active practical scientist with "high sights" on turbojet design. He had planned to design a 5 or 6 stage, 1.5 fuel rate, 100 man-hour, sheetmetal, expendable turbojet with 500 kilo thrust for V weapons (or to be jettisoned from aircraft).

(g) Director Bruno Bruckman, Munich.

In charge of **all** aviation development for BMW.

(h) Doctor Donath, Munich.

In charge of production in all BMW Munich-area plants, (rockets, jets, and reciprocating engines) **except** the Allach Plant No. 2, which was a 1,000,000 square foot layout.

(i) Doctor Dorls, Munich.

In charge of production of BMW 801 in Allach Plant No. 2.

(j) Alfred Bayer, Purchasing and Subcontracting Manager at Eisenach.

Figure 3. Doctor Oestrich (foreground).

2. Executive Personnel (j) (cont'd)

"Slated" by Director in Chief Shaaf to be Materiels Control Man for the entire company. Formerly manager of operations for the North Lloyd Deutsche Lufthausa A.G. Berlin, and once had an office in Room 3408-595 Madison Avenue, New York City; tried to conduct negotiations with the United States for Trans-Atlantic Airmail Transport to Europe and South America.

(k) Personnel Not Located.

(1) Dr. Ulsamer, manager of Berlin and Stassfurt production.
(2) Director Fiedler, in charge of automotive development.
(3) Director Scholl, "Business-Financial Manager"
(4) Doctor Zborowski, in charge of rocket development; an ardent Nazi and Storm Trooper.

3. History.

(a) The BMW was organized to build automobiles of which limited numbers were built during the war at Eisenach. They entered the aircraft engine field as licensees of the Pratt and Whitney "Hornet" and later copied the "Wasp" which evolved into the BMW 132, a nine (9) cylinder air-cooled radial engine used earlier in the war by Dornier in the DO 18L Seaplane (2 radial engines - one fore and one aft), the DO 24 seaplane (3 tractor engines), DO 217 (2 engine) and a number of Junker planes starting with JU 46, JU 52, and progressing through the JU 86K (two engine), JU 90 (four engine) and JU 160 (single engine) transports. It was also used in the FW 200-Condor (four engine) transport.

(b) The principal War time production was the BMW 801 engine, a 14 cylinder, 2 bank, air-cooled radial engine of 42 liter displacement (approximately 2750 cu.in.). This series was in production in a multitude of models and was used principally in volume on the JU 88 (Mostly Night Fighters) and the FW 190A which is shown in Figure #4.

(c) The latest 801 model was the "I" model shown in Figure #5. It was designed for the JU 88 and consisting of a complete "power egg" including a large and compactly integrated turbo supercharger (Figure #6), estimated by General Electric technicians to

3. History (c) (cont'd.)

give sea level performance at 12,000 meters altitude without ram. The "power eggs" were delivered on quick change stands completely cowled and with cooling fans installed ready to "Slap onto the airplane". Production manhours (not including carburetor, pump and supercharger) aggregated approximately 2,000.

(d) In 1934/5 the BMW company initiated a TL (turbojet) development and after working intermittently for five years produced the 003, which went to the test stand in 1939. Progress on the turbojet was slow prior to 1939, due chiefly to the divergent and competing interests of a dual rotation 28 cylinder (model 803) engine, two different models of 27 cylinders each (models 804 and 805), and a 48 cylinder development designated as the BMW 809.

(e) According to Director Schaaf, the Air Department in Berlin was not sure of the success of the turbojets until early in 1944. Henkle had designed and built a turbojet and a turbojet aircraft in 1938 and various "assist" installations had been flown in 1939. The Henkle work had considerable influence upon the BMW design which was originally laid out for 600 kilo thrust at 540 kilo weight. By 1944, however, the thrust and weight had increased to 850 and 570 kilos, respectively.

(f) The first production article on the BMW 003 turbojet was known as Model A-1 and was delivered from the Zuelsdorf (near Berlin) plant early in 1944.

(g) Approximately 450 BMW 003 A-1 (under wing support) and E-1 (over fuselage support) units were built in all. A number of aircraft had been prototyped but the bulk of the production of 003 units was scheduled for installation in large numbers of H-162 aircraft (Figures 7, 8, and 9 taken at the Rheims Airport at Munich).

(h) The ARADO 234 Fighter-Bomber, built in 1944 with two Junker 004 jets (Figure No. 10), had unsatisfactory performance and was scheduled to go to four (two side by side) 003 A-2 units and to be built at a rate of 100/150 per month.

(i) The 003 A-2 and E-2 models were just starting in production, incorporating late improvements in "bucket" design, and had not yet been in the air. The 11 September 1944 schedule called for the combined peak production of 6,000 BMW 003 Models A-2 and E-2, plus spare parts. This peak, which was scheduled to be attained by January 1946, exceeded the

Figure 4. FW 190A.

Figure 5. "I" Model.

Figure 6. Turbo Supercharger.

Figure 7. H-162, known as the "Volksjaeger"

Figure 8. H-162, known as the "Volksjaeger".

Figure 9. H-162, known as the "Volksjaeger".

Figure 10. ARADO 234 Fighter-Bomber.

3. History (1) (cont'd.)

Junker 004 jet peak of 5,000 and 2,000 per month of the 003 jets were to be produced in the slave-operated M-Werke in Nordhausen. This program was later reduced due to bombings.

(j) The company claimed to have started its liquid rocket research in the "Spring of 1943" under the impetus of the March 1943 bombings. They had three major rocket projects, consisting of the 548, 558 and the 718, the latter of which was a rocket to assist the 003 jet.

(k) The 548 was a four wing spiral rocket shot from an aircraft and controlled by wire. Of these, approximately 500 were built (fuselage by Ruhrstahl A.G. of Brackwede) and the production program for the country was between 5,000 and 10,000 per month, according to Dr. Donath, who seemed slightly skeptical of such large numbers.

(l) Rocket No. 558 used in the HS-117 wireless controlled flak rocket was started in May 1943. 150/200 were built while the "K" program, or official schedule, was to be 3,000 per month by October 1945.

(m) Only about 10 or 15 No. 718 assist rockets for 003R turbojets were built. However, the directors of the company had high hopes for this product which contained a pump driven by a shaft connected to the 003 turbojet accessory drive and calculated to give 1250 kilos additional thrust with a fuel consumption of 5.5 lbs. of fuel per 1000 pounds of thrust per second. This design was started in the summer of 1943.

4. Future Plans.

(a) The managers of BMW were all proud that their company was the only one in Germany that built "all three", viz. conventional, turbojets and rocket power plants.

(b) There was a continuing program for increasing the thrust and improving the 003-A2 which was **not** yet "fool proof". Most of the refinements of this design had been done in 1941 and it is to be emphasized that the experience of the last two years **had not** yet been incorporated in the A-2 model.

(c) The demand for higher power turbojets resulted in the 018 design which had a maximum thrust and weight of 3500 kilos and 2900 kilos respectively. Figure 11 shows the only 018 believed ever to have been completely assembled. It was destroyed by the enemy before evacuating Stassfurt.

4. Future Plans (Cont'd.)

(d) The 018 components were to be used in a gas turbine known as the 028.

(e) Storm Trooper Zborowski was not located in Munich and production of liquid rockets was not advanced sufficiently for the investigator to obtain a clear picture of liquid rocket plans except as described heretofore. Samples and designs however, will be shipped to the United States, where the design will be analysed by experts.

5. Production, Engineering and Design Limitations.

(a) The Bureau of Aeronautics and its contractors might learn a lot from the BMW experience with the 003 turbojet. In comparing this unit with current American and English units, the following factors should be weighed:

(1) The 003 was **actually** in production and flying combat aircraft.
(2) It was a ten (10) year old design.
(3) According to directives from the Air Ministry, this engine **had to be** built with three (3) serious limitations outside of performance:

   a. It must be produced in not over 500 man hours per unit.
   b. It could not use over 0.6 kilos of nickel per unit. (Most of the nickel came from Finland.)
   c. It must be broken down into the maximum number of easy-to-manufacture components and must be easily accessible for field maintenance.

(b) Engineer Dr. Oestrich, with a staff of assistants and specialists, was the designer of the 003 unit; but before a production program was embarked upon, Dr. Fattler, with his assistants, was given the design to rationalize so that 500 man hours would be the manufacturing limit. This necessitated extensive use of sheetmetal parts, and Fattler with his American automotive experience was a "natural" to supervise this effort. According to both Oestrich and Fattler, interrogated independently in Stassfurt and Eisenach, there were long and acrimonious conferences but

Figure 11.

5. Production, Engineering and Design Limitations (b) (cont'd.)

out of these conferences came a final meeting of minds with production distributed as follows:

Machine Work	220 man hours
Sheetmetal Work	160 man hours
Starter, regulator and miscel	80 man hours
Assembly	40 man hours
Total	500 man hours

(c) Since vanes and buckets are used in large numbers, special attention was devoted to the design and production of these elements. The 003 turbine buckets (of which there were 77 in Model A-1, but 66 in A and E-2) were fabricated from strip sheet stock in ten (10) high speed cutting and drawing operations. (A-1 used metric 2.15 gage, while A-2 went up to 2.65 stock). Most of the turbine buckets were made in Geislungen, (in Wurttenburg between Stuttgart and Ulm) by the I.G. "W.M.F.", and were the least available components requiring a special alloy of 16% Chromium "band steel" furnished by Bohler in Kapfenberg. Figures 12 and 13 show production steps on 003 A-2 turbine buckets; Figure 14 shows the internal bucket shroud.

(d) Nozzles were tooled to meter fuel within 1-1/2 percent and apparently no difficulties were experienced, and it was unnecessary to match nozzle sets, as in American I-16 practice.

(e) The A-2 had more improvements for production than for performance. <u>In all models the turbine wheels could be rapidly inspected and changed on an airplane in two (2) hours.</u> (This was not a feature of the JU 004). 50 percent complete turbine wheel assemblies were procured with 100 percent spare buckets.

(f) The planned percentage of spare installation units had not been firmly established but was believed to have been 40 to 50 percent on the AR 234 and was tentatively planned at only 20 percent for the Volksjaeger (H-162) which was light in weight (5480 lbs. gross) and cost, and constructed of non-critical materials.

(g) Figures 15, 16 and 17 show how Volksjaegers were produced ahead

5. Production, Engineering and Design Limitations (g) (cont'd.)

of jets and dispersed in "farm buildings" where wings and jets could be later attached. Dispersals of this nature were located in the vicinity of Bernburg.

6. Summary of Technical Highlights of BMW turbojet Design.

(a) 003 A-2 turbojet.

(1) **Performance of Jet:**

Static Thrust: 850 kilo @ 9500 rpm.
Weight: 570 kilos (from documents, but more likely 600 to 610 according to officials).
Dimensions: 69 cm. x 3.6 meters.
One turbine stage with 66 buckets.
Seven compressor stages.
Fuel Rate: Approximately 1.25 (?).
Oil Rate: 1.0 kilo per hr. (Spec. was 4.0).
(Figure 18, taken in the basement of the Durhoff Plant shows several of the manufacturing details.)
(Figure 19 and 20 show details of enemy destroyed 003's.)

(2) **Materiels:**

Compressor blades: Electron in early stages with Dural in later stages.
Combustion chamber: Medium carbon steel, aluminum coated.
Nozzles: Sichromal.
Tail Cone: Carbon steel except spider, which was sichromal.

(3) **Miscellaneous Detail:**

Starter (In circuit with two spark plugs): 2 cylinder, 2 cycle motor, 7½ HP, same as JU 004 (Riedelstarter).

Figure 12.

Figure 13.

Figure 14.

Figure 15.

Figure 16.

Figure 17.

Figure 18.

Figure 19.

Figure 20.

6. Summary of Technical Highlights of BMW turbojet Design (a)(3)(cont'd)

    Fuel Pump: Max Pressure 90 atmosphere.
    Combustion Efficiency: 90/95% S.L. with almost no loss of pressure from combustion to turbine entry.
    Compressor % Efficiency: 80%
    Turbine % Efficiency: 75/80%
    Maximum Turbine Blade T°:   700° C.

This engine has been run up to 1200 Kilo thrust. A-1 had a life of 50 hours but this was being rapidly increased. Turbines were inspected every ten (10) hours.

    (4) Performance of Type 162 Jet fighter with one 003 A-2 turbojet:

        V Max S.L.:   800 K/hr. (490 m/hr.)
              19,700 ft.:   840 K/hr. (520 m/hr.)
        R of C. S.L.:   4230 ft./min.
              19,700 ft.:   2460 ft./min.
        Time to climb to 19,700 ft.:   6.6 min.
        No wind T.O. run: 1200 meters (?)
        Ceiling @ mean weight: 39,400 ft.
        Full throttle range, S.L. normal fuel: 135 miles.

    (5) Performance of AR 234 with four (4) 003 A-2 Turbojets:

        Flying weight: 8450 kilo.
        R/C sealevel: 28 meters/sec.
        Speed @ 10 km.:   883 km./hr.
        Range @ 10/13 km.:   1400 km.

  (b)   018 Turbojet (Figure 11).

    (1) Performance:

        Maximum Thrust: 3400/3500 kilos.
        Weight: 2900 kilo.
        Fuel Rate claimed:   1.08 #/#Thr/hr.

6. Summary of Technical Highlights of BMW turbojet Design (b)(cont'd)

(2) **Details - Illustrated in Figures 11, 21, 22, 23, 24, 25, 26, 27, 28, 29 and 30:**

Compressor stages: 12 (Figures 11, 21, 22, and 23).
Compressor shaft bearings: 2
Turbine Stages: 3 (not found).
Approximate diameter of shaft: $5\frac{1}{4}"$
Number of Burners: 24 (see Figures 29 and 30).
Approximate size of main ball bearings: 0.7" diameter
(See Figure 29)

(3) Miscellaneous note: This was the only 018 ever assembled. It was located in a surface crater near the Stassfurt underground factory and as indicated by the photographs was destroyed before the town was captured.

(4) Performance of 018 in an aircraft design - P-122 Henschel. This was to be a two (2) seater flying wing as per sketch.

Figure 21.

Figure 22.

Figure 23.

Figure 24.

Figure 25.

Figure 26.

Figure 27.

Figure 28.

Figure 29.

Figure 30.

6. Summary of Technical Highlights of BMW turbojet Design (b)(4)(cont'd)

Flying Weight:	15,100 Kilo (33,300 lbs.)
R/C:	57 M/sec.
Speed S.L.:	1010 K/hr. (627 M/hr.)
Speed 37,000:	935 K/hr. (581 M/hr.)
Range @ 17 Kilo Alt.:	2000 Kilo (1242 miles).
@ 10 Kilo Alt.:	1110 Kilo.

(5) Progress of 018 Turbo design. The development of the 018 had been seriously set back by strategic bombing. The operation had been moved four (4) different times, the last move being to the salt mine at Stassfurt. It was originally scheduled to fly in December 1944.

(c) 028 PTL (Propellor Gas Turbine).

(1) Performance:

H.P. at S.L. to airscrew:	7,700
H.P. of Jet at 900 kilo/hr.:	6,300
Weight:	3500 Kg.
Fuel Consumption (Max.):	3700 Kg/hr.
Prop Speed:	900 rpm.
Shaft Speed:	5000 rpm.

(NOTE: Drawings and some specifications of the 003 A-1, -2, and E-2, the 018 and the 028 were located in underground salt mine and in a container buried in a forest near Stassfurt. These documents are now in the possession of CIOS and will be available to BuAer).

7. Production Trends.

(a) The Germans changed their programs frequently; these changes were often of a radical nature, necessitated by strategic bombing. For example, Director Bruckman reported that one raw material of the 003 jet was changed seven (7) times without any concession on economy or performance.

(b) In 1937, when the Durhoff and Allach plants were planned, the Air Ministry was petitioned, at the instigation of a BMW engineering group that pointed out the eventual danger of bombing, and it was sug-

7. Production Trends (b) (cont'd)

gested that the entire expansion be placed underground in salt mines. No action was taken and 2,000,000 square feet of floor space were built in 1938 through 1943. Figure 31 shows the Durhoff plant which consisted of eleven (11) buildings on the side of a large hill, well camouflaged by trees that grew within five (5) inches of the walls giving excellent cover.

(c) Figure 32 shows the latest type of **parabolic** roofed building as constructed in 1943 in both Durhoff and Allach. These plants had superior (sawdust base) tile floors. The Durhoff plant was first hit by bombs in February 1944, and as of March 1945, there were no plans for its conversion or repair, as it was too fallible.

(d) The decision to move CO3 production underground was sold to Minister Speer in March 1944, and was finally put in motion in May 1944, after the big fighter plants had been badly bombed. Mine space was assigned by the Minister of Production and the Air Ministry. Test cells were to be dispersed into small buildings at least a kilo from the mine shafts.

(e) Until early in 1944 the German Air Force was not sure of the eventual success of turbojet propelled aircraft. Both BMW and Junkers were convinced of the trend, and Colonel Knehmeyer, chief of the development end of the Air Ministry, was really the man most responsible for the decision to go to jets on all VF. The final higher authority decision was made in September 1944. The changeover, however, was to be accomplished with a minimum loss of production with the M-Werke (Nordhausen) and many subcontractors assisting, including the VDM propellor plants in Frankfort and Marklissa.

(f) One of the most serious problems in making salt mines available was the inefficiency of the elevator equipment which belatedly was being rebuilt, speeded up, and increased in capacity. Figure 33 shows the "Lift H ouse" at Springen (near Eisenach). Figure 34 shows the old (left) and start of new (right) lift construction at Stassfurt. The small size and slowness of the elevators placed serious limitations on machine tool size and especially handicapped the start and efficiency of the Stassfurt operation. The underground Springen plant was originally planned to start producing "by Christmas". Actually only 500 tools were in place, and not all of these were yet in operation.

Figure 31.

Figure 32.

Figure 33.

Figure 34.

8. **Salt Mines as Factories.**

(a) Corridors vary from ten (10) to thirty (30) meters in width. Access is usually inadequate and except in "drift" mines, is a serious bottleneck. The humidity is low (around 20%) and great care had to be taken not to "melt" the walls by evaporation of excessive moisture in cement that was being poured. The only corrosion problem seemed to be in the lifts and vertical shafts due to high moisture content.

(1) The Springen mines, (the largest of three mines in the Eisenach area), contained 1,900,000 square feet of usable space assigned to BMW. It was to operate three (3) eight-hour shifts with 6,000 employees. 55 percent were slaves and <u>less than</u> 100 women in all. The heavy pressing equipment from Town Werke in Eisenach was to go underground and was to be supplemented by additional sheet metal equipment to have a total capacity of 3,000 sets of steel parts per month. Since other operations were only tooled for 2,000 per month, there was a 50 percent safety factor in the sheet metal equipment.

(2) A similar policy was followed in the M-Werke at Nordhausen. Figure 35 was taken in the Nordhausen mine and shows the enclosed V-1 assembly line to the left with storage space above. The Nordhausen plant was originally scheduled to build two thousand 003 turbojets per month and to fabricate various percentages of different components. By March 1945, their assembly peak was 800 per month.

(3) The Stassfurt plant was the Berlin (Spandau and Zulsdorf) dispersal. It made no sheet metal parts but was confined to machining, design and test. The underground factory had three levels at 400, 430 and 460 meters, respectively. The first was assigned to 003, the second to 003 screw machine, and other small parts. The lowest level was "independently" operated by "Walser Werke" of the Fisher Company which had rushed its ball bearing machinery into this mine after the bombing of their Sweinfurt plant.

(4) The preponderance of German Industrial opinion was that there were enough mines in existence in Germany to house practically all German aircraft industry, but as BMW Director Bruckman expressed it, "the best dispersal is a strong Luftwaffe". Figure 36 shows typical damage sustained by the Munich main plant producing BMW 801 type engines.

RESTRICTED

9. Test Stands.

BMW had a total of forty (40) conventional engine test stands of which sixteen (16) were in Durhoff and twenty-four (24) in Munich (six (6) of which were out of commission due to bombing). Their capacity was up to 3000 H.P. The BMW 801 engines were originally tested six (6) hours green run, which was later cut to $2\frac{1}{2}$ hours. Final run was one hour maximum, but was cut to around 15 minutes near the end. Turbo-jet stands were dispersed, and of simple brick and concrete construction. Figures 2, 37, 38 and 39 show details, while instrumentation is shown in Figures 40 and 41. A liquid rocket stand is shown in Figure 42 taken at Allach.

10. Employment Policy.

(a) Employees:

```
Eisenach and Dispersals .......... 8,000
Berlin Dispersals ................15,000
Munich and Dispersals ............30,000
```

(Of this, the Allach plants employed 17,000 to 18,000 of which 3,000 were Germans, 13,000 "slaves", and 1,300 German technicians). It is evident that the company had little control over the manpower allocation, and took such labor as was allocated from Berlin.

(b) Hours of labor varied from eight (8) to twelve (12) per day, increasing as the going became tougher. Managers expressed opinions that eight (8) hours per day was the practical daily limit for a man to work in a salt mine.

11. Production Schedules.

(a) These were established by Lt. General Kessler and were known as "K" programs. General Kessler was formerly President of the Bergman Electric Company in Berlin, and was originally commissioned to disperse and re-establish ball bearing production after the bombing of Sweinfurt, which he was said to have effectively accomplished in three (3) months. Kessler was made responsible for the production of "V" weapons, the Volksjaeger (H-162) and jets.

Figure 35.

Figure 36.

Figure 37.

Figure 38.

Figure 39.

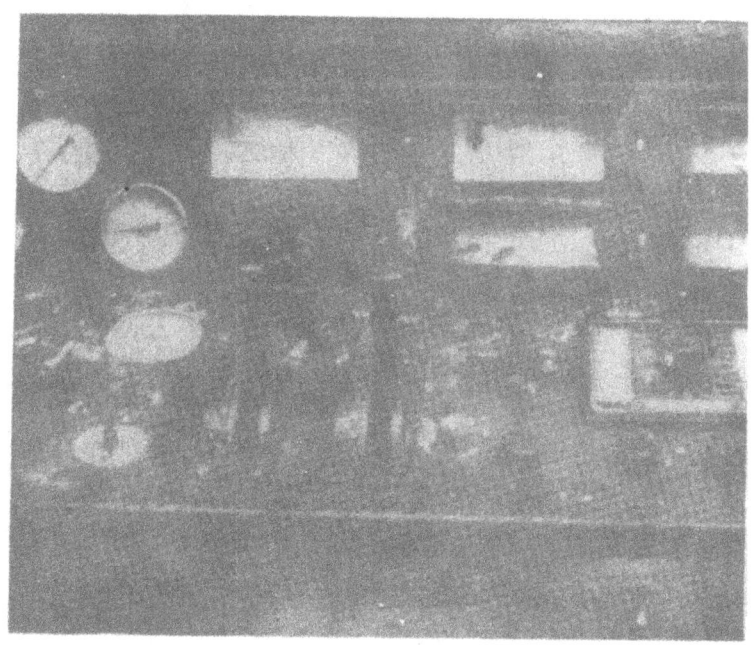

Figure 40.

Figure 41.

Figure 42.

11. Production Schedules (cont'd.)

(1) The investigators located the "K" program and production planning chart for the 003 turbojets; this chart showed the original (11 September 1944) 6,000 per month schedule with several successive reductions and delays which came as a result of bombing, the necessity for manufacturing conversion parts, and over-optimism at the Air Ministry.

(2) BMW 003 Original Park Schedule (9-11-44).

Incl. S-Werke

	MODEL A-1	MODEL A & E-2	"VILLAGE" SERIES	TOTAL
November 1944	75			75
December 1944	100			100
January 1945	150		30	180
February 1945	150	50	200	400
March 1945	150	150	500	800
April 1945	150	400	850	1400
May 1945	150	750	1000	1900
June 1945	115	1250	1000	2365
July 1945		1800	1000	2800
August 1945		2350	1000	3350
September 1945		3100	1000	4100
October 1945		3700	1000	4700
November 1945		4300	1000	5300
December 1945		4750	1000	5750
January 1946		5000	1000	6000

Raw material to be scheduled three (3) months ahead of assembly.

(3) Revised 003 program of 8 March 1945, broken down into Plants:

1945	Zulsdorf & Stassfurt A-1	Eisenach & A-E-2	Springen A-E-2	"Villages" A-3-2	BMW Total	M-Werke Total	Grand Total
March	180		20		200		200
April	150		100	100	350		350
May	150	50	250	200	650	20	670
June	150	150	400	300	1000	80	1080
July	150	300	550	500	1500	200	1700
August		500	700	500	1700	400	2100
September					1700	800	2500

"The above schedules were for the final delivery of assembled units. The raw materials were to be procured so that they are on hand at the works three (3) months ahead of the program".

"The above is a transcript of the "Lieferprogram fur gerat 003".

12. Junker 004 vs. BMW 003.

(a) The JU 004 turbojet was ahead of the BMW from a production standpoint, with approximately 6000 built with a peak month in March 1945, producing 1050; this compares with a total of only 450 BMW 003's in all. In spite of being behind in total production, the Air Ministry recognized the superior accessibility, reduced weight, material and labor cost with improved thrust-weight ratio and higher eventual thrust possibilities of the 003. This was the reason for scheduling a 6000 peak compared with a 5000 peak on the JU 004.

(b) After the heavy bombings of March 1945, future plans were shelved, larger jets cancelled, and a frantic attempt was made to increase the ME 262 aircraft production, resulting in priority being given to the JU 004 jet (which took at least 700 manhours to produce).

12. Junker 004 vs. BMW 003 (cont'd.)

(c) Table of comparison between the JU 004 and BMW 003 turbojets:

	BMW 003	JU 004
Maximum design thrust	850 kilo	900 kilo*
Weight	600 kilo	760 kilo
RPM	9500	8700
Fuel Rate	1.25.(?)	1.32

(*Note: The 004-C was to start in production in May and attain a peak by July 1945, and was to have 1000 kilo thrust.)

13. Government Supervision.

(a) An annual accounting was made on standard forms. Inspection was by company personnel with a Luftwaffe office in each area, like BuAer's B.A.R., but somewhat less extensive. For example, in Eisenach there was one Flight Engineer (equivalent in rank to a Lt. Comdr.), four (4) assisting officers and four (4) civilian inspectors. All aluminum and magnesium were allocated from Berlin, but there was little evidence of steel allocation to any end product.

(b) Screening of machine tools: the Germans never seemed to be short of machine tools and used a great deal of duplicate tooling. Cost seemed to be no object, but designs were such that universally standard tools could be used. Some French machines had been removed to Germany and were used to supplement their production capacity.

14. Items of Miscellaneous Interest.

(a) **Forged Cylinder Heads.** These were investigated in 1938, but were abandoned "for cost and metallurgical reasons".

(b) **Impellers.** These were purchased from firms such as I.G. Farben, Bitterfeld that <u>pressed them to shape</u> from cooky-shaped billets. Figure 43 shows the 801 turbo supercharger impeller. It is built in two pieces, the curved entrance being separately fabricated.

Figure 43.

14. Items of Miscellaneous Interest (cont'd.)

(c) <u>Cylinder Finning</u>. The BMW 801 cylinder finning is both ingenious and economical and in some quarters conceded to be a great improvement over the Wright "W-fin" design. The cylinder barrel exterior is machined with a fine spirally cut female buttress thread into which is rolled and locked an aluminum spiral fin .04" x 1" ribbon.

(d) <u>16 Kilometer Altitude Test Chamber</u>. BMW had a tremendous altitude cold chamber in Munich capable of temperatures down to -50/55° C. This test house was imbedded in solid concrete and was sometimes used by Junkers.

(e) <u>Solid Cement Factories</u>. In an effort to combat the strategic bombing, BMW built a heavy steel reinforced solid concrete block house at Allach. This was never completed due to "lack of cement".

(f) The BMW 801 engine had a <u>cast steel crankshaft</u>, and the link rods and master rods were shot peened. There was no vibration dampener on the BMW 801.

(g) BMW was making progress on the "idiot's control", an automatic flight engineer or "Kommandogerat" controlling manifold pressure, spark, supercharger setting, shifting or control, fuel injection and prop speed setting all automatically.

15. <u>Conclusion</u>. There were four (4) leading aircraft engine and jet producers in Germany. This semi-technical report has endeavored to cover the history, layout and objectives of the Bavarian Motor Works (BMW) as representing one of the most progressive of the four. The outstanding lesson that BuAer can learn from this company is (1) the time and cost required for development of new power plants, (2) the importance of good production engineering geared to universal equipment. <u>Make "Designs that can be built"</u>.

Prepared by:

H.C. HASKELL,
Cmdr., USNR.

BAYERISCHE MOTOR WERKE (BMW)

12 May, 19 June 1945

Reported By

Dr. H. A. LIEBHAFSKY, U. S., ORD.
Mr. R. H. NORRIS, U. S. ORD.
Mr. E. H. HULL, U. S. ORD.

CIOS Target Number 5/74

Jet Propulsion

COMBINED INTELLIGENCE OBJECTIVES SUB-COMMITTEE
G-2 Division, SHAEF (Rear), APO 413

The Naval & Military Press Ltd

TABLE OF CONTENTS

SUBJECT **PAGE NO.**

   I. Target Location 3

  II. Subject Covered 3

 III. Summary 3

  IV. Report 3

   V. Photo Titles 6

Figure 1
  Sketch of Test Pit

BAYERISCHE MOTOR WERKE (BMW)
Target No. 5/74

I. TARGET LOCATION (Sheet M49 at 11274811)

The main entrance to the BMW plant is 6 km. SSE of Dachau and 0.7 km. SSE of Karlsfeld on the west side of the Munich road. The rocket motor test pits are in the SE corner of the plant.

II. SUBJECT COVERED

Liquid fuel rocket motor testing installation and associated shops.

III. SUMMARY

This report covers an inspection made about 12 May by Lt. Col. G. J. Gollin (British), Squad Leader E. J. A. Kenny (British), 1st Lt. Ozel (U. S., Ord.), and H. A. Liebhafsky (U. S. T/O) of CIOS No. 183 and a later trip made by R. H. Norris and E. H. Hull (U. S. T/O) on 19 June 1945.

The target contains an important rocket motor testing station, briefly described below, which might be studied further if the German operators could be obtained for explanations in order to answer certain questions concerning methods of measurement and operation, safety precautions, reasons for explosions, test results, etc.

IV. REPORT

There is no doubt that the target is one of the outstanding German stations for stationary tests on rocket motors. Stations of comparable importance seem to have been only at Peenemunde and Berlin.

Our first party was conducted through the station by Dr. Hemesath, chief chemist of BMW for rocket fuels, who claims to be the inventor of hypergole fuels utilizing nitric acid as oxidant. He claims further that some 6000 rocket-fuel combinations have been tested at the target. Nitric acid was the only oxidant used in these tests; many reducing agents (fuels) were tried, the choice of these being dictated largely by supply considerations. Hydrogen peroxide has been studied for submarine purposes in the laboratory, but never in a rocket motor.

The station was begun early in 1943. It was to consist of 12 pairs of test pits, each pair having one control room. Most of these pits were built, but not all were operated.

Thrust was measured hydraulically through a membrane. There was also an electrical method of thrust measurement, but this did not involve a quartz crystal; a reasonable guess is that it involved changing the capacity of a condenser by a mechanical displacement proportional to the thrust. (The CIOS team expects to clear up this matter and to obtain samples of the thrust-measuring devices). The reactants are delivered by pressurizing, air or nitrogen being used. Reaction is begun by having an explosive rupture of a metal membrane, which starts the flow of reactants. (Lt. Col. Gollin says that he is thoroughly familiar with this method, which he uses). The hypergoles are self-igniting; for the ether fuels, ignition by means of gunpowder, by means of an electric spark, and by means of hypergoles in small quantity has been used.

Although pressurized tanks, see Photo No. 1, filled by means of electrically driven portable pumps, were used for reactant supply, a more elegant system was practically complete. Four sets of large metal acid tanks and smaller fuel tanks were suspended on scales for accurate weighing. Pipes led from these tanks to a pipe tunnel passing under the floor of the test pits for distribution of the reactants. The acid tanks are cylindrical in shape and laid horizontally on their weighing apparatus (See Photo No. 3). Acid tanks held about 750 gals. and the fuel tanks, 200 gals., approximately.

Apparently no precautions have been taken to keep the reactant systems separate. Fuel and acid tanks are located in the same room and the supply pipes lead through the same duct. There is no visible protection for these supply lines in the test pits and apparently no means of keeping blast or fire from travelling along the pipe tunnel from one pit to the next, or to the tank rooms.

Exhaust gases from the motor tests are taken care of in an elaborate duct system. A long horizontal brick duct, 5 x 7 ft. inside, is built parallel to the row of test pits. At each pit a short brick section, built at right angles to the main duct, ends in an open-ended telescoping steel tube about 4 ft. in diameter, as shown in Photo No. 4. Exhaust gases collected by this tube run along the horizontal duct to a vertical stack about 50 ft. high, up which they are forced by a centrifugal fan. There is a gate valve in each individual test stand duct. Some of these side ducts have built beside them a brick observation room for looking axially into the rocket motor from the exhaust end.

As mentioned above the test pits are built in pairs with a common observation room between each pair. There are sections between these units for workrooms and the reactant storage spaces. The test pits, 13 x 20 x 12 ft. high, are enclosed by 30-inch concrete walls except on the front, which is covered by a rolling steel door to be opened during tests. Steel T-slots are built into the floor and walls to facilitate fastening equipment. Excellent lighting is provided by lamps near the ceiling covered by safety glass, some of which has been cracked by explosions. Photo No. 5 is a general view of one of these test pits showing the stand for mounting the rocket and measuring thrust on the right and on the left reading from bottom to top, a reactant supply pipe, observation window, wire screen for the window, the screen being raised at the time the picture was taken, and two lights. In the far corner an entrance door can be seen standing open. This leads into a vestibule opening into the observation room, the test pit on the other side of that room, and to the outside. The T-slots in the floor and walls can be seen also. Each pair of test pits opens on the exhaust side into a paved yard divided by walls at the sides and enclosed by the duct at the rear.

Two long windows lead from each observation room to each test pit (shown in Fig. 1). The glass in these windows contains 4 laminations totaling 2" in thickness. In one of the pits a severe explosion had spalled the concrete walls and cracked the outer glass window but nothing penetrated. Photo No. 5 shows an investigator holding this cracked window. Spalling of the concrete wall between the two windows and above the nearer can be seen as well. During tests these windows are covered by a heavy wire screen which was missing from the cracked window, probably having been removed for repair. The space between the two pieces of glass is either heated electrically or dried with a dehydrating agent to insure non-fogging.

Explosions are not uncommon since nitric acid tends to form explosive organic nitrates if oxidation of the fuel does not proceed rapidly in mixing.

The observation rooms are equipped with neat control boards mounted under the observation windows as well as a large instrument panel which appeared to be arranged for movie photography. On this panel were 2 tachometers, a clock, several pressure gauges and 2 temperature indicators.

Some of the test pits appeared to be arranged for testing the entire propulsion unit of the Henschel 8-117 including tanks. This assumption is strengthened by the fact that several partially destroyed 117 power plants were seen nearby. Also in the shop across the street from the test pits were found several 117 tanks, pistons and a burned-out combustion pot. Experiments were also made in motors of the X-4 type in which the reactant rate is 0.8 kg/sec. for 20 sec. duration. Work has been done on ATO units for rocket planes on a 10 times larger scale than the above, as well as for longer times. Specific impulses of 200 sec. are claimed but this point has not been verified.

Dr. Homesath feels that nitric acid is the most promising of all oxidants for rocket purposes. He admits, however, that no operational use has yet been made of it in Germany but says there have been trial flights. Most experiments were made with a 5 to 1 ratio of nitric acid to fuel which indicates an excess of acid.

V. **PHOTO TITLES**

1. Pressurised reactant tank suspended for weighing.
2. Acid supply tank mounted on scales.
3. Fuel supply tank suspended for weighing.
4. Exhaust gas telescoping duct.
5. General view of a test pit.
6. A pit in which an explosion had occurred.

Photo No. 1

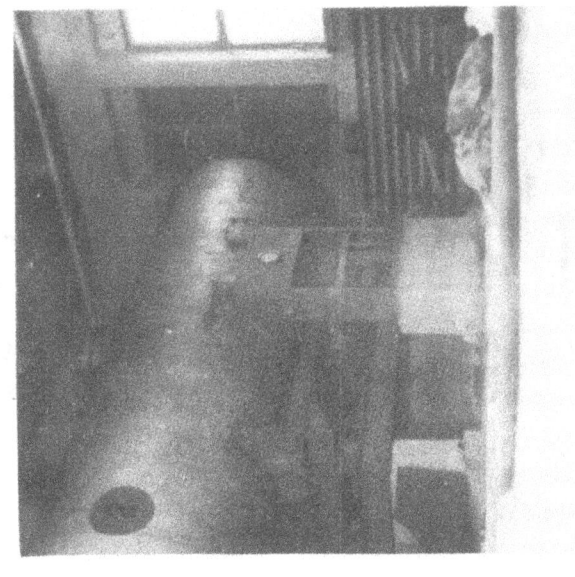

Photo No. 2

Photo No. 4

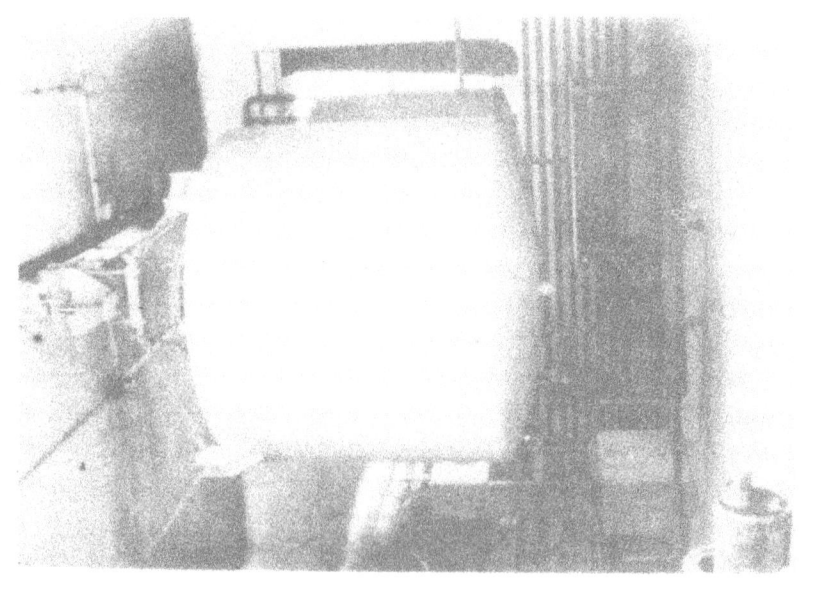

Photo No. 3

Photo No. 5

Photo No. 6

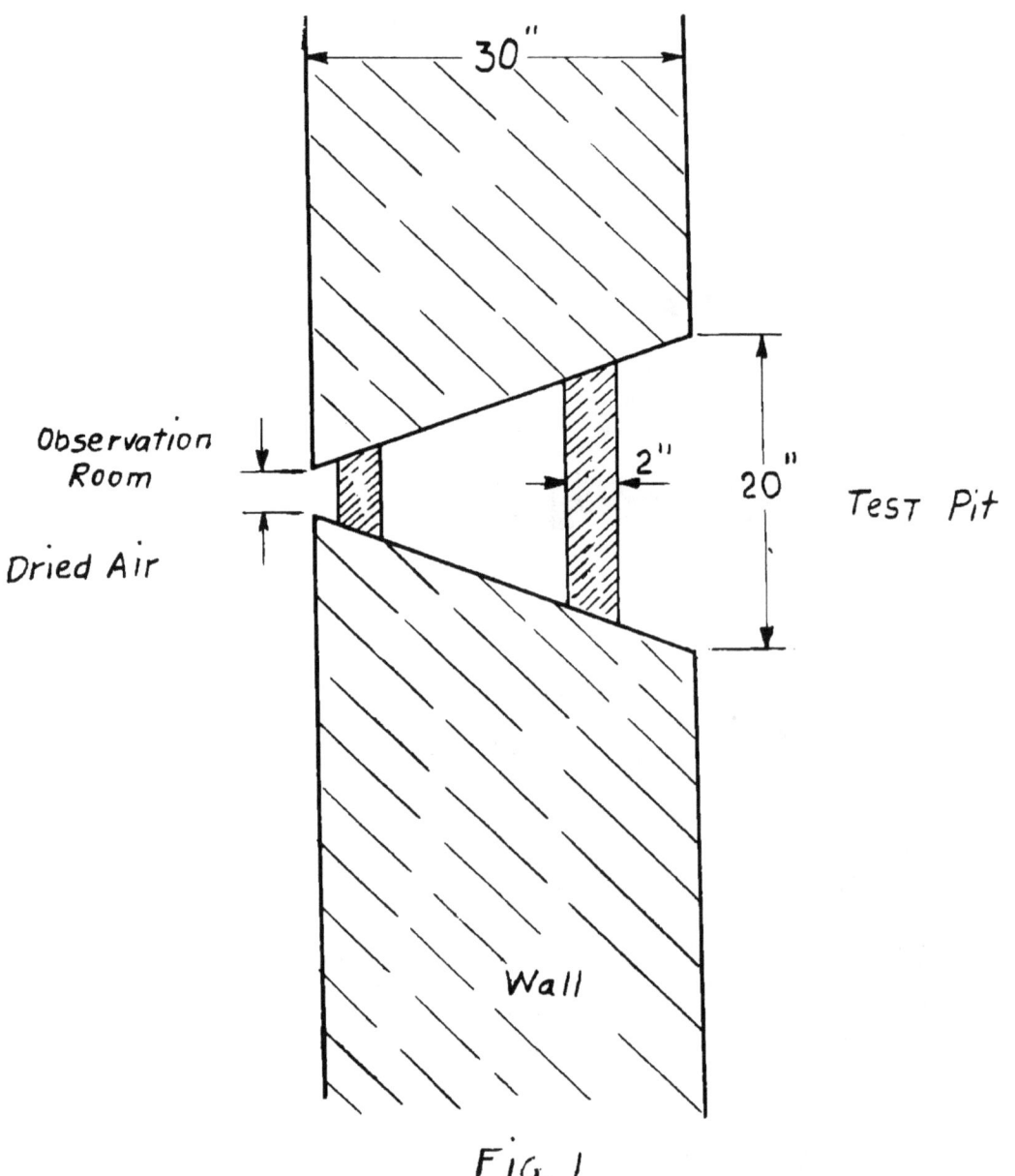

Fig. 1

www.ingramcontent.com/pod-product-compliance
Lightning Source LLC
Chambersburg PA
CBHW081330190426
43193CB00044B/2902